Augie's Adventure in the City

by Edward L. Nadel

Illustrated by Tzvi Kogan

Dedicated to:

My honey, Penny, I couldn't do this without you.

To Rachael and Josh, you have been with me throughout this adventure and have been my inspiration.

And many, many thanks to all who contributed your time and comments to me. It is so appreciated.

A very special thanks to Tzvi Kogan, my illustrator who has helped to make this book come alive!

Chapter 1

There he is, happy as a butterfly on a sunny day, walking through the forest enjoying every step of the way. Look, he's sniffing each and every flower, some even twice. We know how slowly turtles move, don't we? Well, Augie is no different. Augie is really a sweet and handsome young brown turtle who likes to have fun. On his walk this terrific day, Augie met Defer and Hotie, the donkey twins. You could always tell who Hotie was; she was the donkey with a pretty pink bow.

"Hi Defer, hi Hotie," Augie said excitedly. Defer and Hotie turned around and saw Augie coming toward them on a winding, grassy path. "Hi Augie, how are you?" they answered together. "It sure is nice to see you. How about a game of tree tag?"

"Sounds like a great idea to me," Augie answered happily. "Can I go first?"

"Sure thing!" Hotie said, "ready, set, go!" Augie ran towards his donkey friends and tried to tag them when they weren't touching a tree. Most of the time Augie lost at tree tag since his friends moved so much faster than he did, but he didn't care if he won or lost. Having a chance to play with his friends was all Augie really cared about.

This time, Augie was running after Hotie trying to tag her. Hotie was running away from Augie and wasn't looking where she was running. She ran smack into her brother Defer and knocked him down. Augie tagged Defer instead.

After playing long and hard, all three of them were tired and hungry. Defer had a great idea. "Why don't we rest for a while and have a snack?" he suggested. Augie, and Hotie readily agreed. Augie had some honey under his shell to share with his two friends. (That's one of the neat things about turtles-they always carry snacks.) Hotie found some flowers to dip into the honey and brought them over. The three enjoyed their feast so much you could hear their UMMMS and AHHHS throughout the forest.

As Augie, Hotie, and Defer were finishing their scrumptious goodies, a newcomer approached. It was Harvey the Inchworm. Harvey was an inquisitive little fellow who always asked a ton of questions- but he almost never gave anyone time to answer them.

"Hi guys, what's going on?" Harvey asked, not waiting for an answer as usual. "Are you playing a game? What game are you playing? Can you use another player?"

Augie was about to reply but he never got the chance.

"It doesn't matter," he continued, "Do you fellas want to take a walk to the new country house over the hill? Some people moved in and they have lots of flowers, and a pool, and kids, and lots and lots of poison ivy, and we can wander around. Poison ivy tickles my nose. It's a shame people have such a terrible time with it." Hotie opened her mouth to say something but again, she never got the chance, either.

"Well do you want to go or not?" Harvey interrupted. "You can finish your game later."

Augie turned from Defer to Hotie with a questioning gaze. Harvey bounced up and down impatiently, waiting for an answer. Finally, the three of them nodded yes to Harvey's invitation. It was settled. They would all go to the new country house over the hill.

Defer collected the leftover flowers and put them back into Augie's shell, while Hotie gathered up the remaining honey and stored it next to the flowers. Then, off they went—Augie, Defer, Hotie, and Harvey—on an adventure they would never forget.

The four friends left the clearing in which they'd been playing and walked in a single file on the grass, through the trees, over the stream, around the rocks, and straight to the top of the hill near the new house.

Chapter 2

All the animals in the forest had watched as the new house was being built. Everything started the previous summer when workmen came with a bulldozer and a backhoe to clear the land for the new house. A few days later, huge trucks arrived carrying load after load of lumber which the workmen used to build the house and more trucks came with bricks for the chimney. As the weather got colder, the workmen did their work inside the house, putting in pipes, electric wires, tiles on the floor, and paint on the walls.

Standing on top of the hill, looking down at the new pretty little grey house with a red brick chimney sitting on top, the four friends could not wait to start exploring. Hotie ran down the hill first quickly followed by her brother. Ever so slowly, Augie followed, with Harvey on Augie's back, getting a free ride.

Defer and Hotie walked up the path to the new house, past rows and rows of tulips and daisies all behind a pretty green fence. "Wow!" Defer exclaimed, "these flowers sure are beautiful... and I bet they taste great too!"

All around the house were cute little bushes, and if there was any space between two bushes, there were more flowers.

A rickety old wheelbarrow filled to overflowing with different colored pansies sat next to the steps leading up to the front door. There were red pansies, pink pansies, purple pansies, and yellow pansies, all seeming to bubble over the edge and hang down with so many blossoms it almost looked as if the wheelbarrow was smiling.

Defer and Hotie walked towards the back of the little grey house, continuing to admire the beautiful flowers as they went. They came upon a green picket fence standing straight and tall that went all the way around to the backyard.

Over the fence, Hotie and Defer saw a happy sight—a swimming pool filled with rubber floats. Behind the pool there were swings and a seesaw.

It took a little while, but Augie finally strolled up with Harvey still on his back. "What's up, fellas?" Harvey chimed in. "What are you looking at?"

"Fun things," Defer answered quickly before Harvey could ask another question. "Well then," Harvey answered, "I'm going to take a closer look." Harvey wriggled down Augie's smooth back, onto Augie's wrinkled knee, then slipped off Augie's knee and landed with a tiny thud onto Augie's toes and rolled onto some soft green grass. After shaking himself off, Harvey inched his way through a hole in the fence.

Just as Augie was thinking that it wasn't such a good idea to go past a locked gate, he noticed Defer nuzzling the latch with his nose. All of a sudden, the latch gave way and the gate swung open. Defer and Hotie trotted inside, leaving Augie behind. Augie thought for a moment and said to himself: Well, I'll be careful not to upset anything, and I'll go in only for a moment. Off he went exploring with his friends.

"What a fun place this is," Harvey said out loud. Everyone walked into the yard very cautiously. Defer and Hotie walked towards the shimmering aquamarine water of the pool and sat down in two very comfortable chairs. They sat in the sunshine with their hooves up, their heads back, and rested as they let the warm rays of the sun bathe them in a golden glow.

All around them and circling the pool were flower pots filled with dozens of red and yellow marigolds that looked like bright buttons. What a beautiful sight!

Augie wanted to wander around and do some exploring. He walked past the swings, past the seesaw, past an old tire hanging from a tree, and found a trail leading away from the house. He came upon what looked like a work area in a small clearing. There were flower pots, shovels, some cute little bushes, and a few holes dug into the ground where the bushes were going to be planted.

As Augie got closer to the largest of the holes, some loose earth began to give way under his weight and he fell into the hole. (He was very lucky to land on his feet since it's nearly impossible for a turtle to get up without help if he's stuck on his back.) Augie stood up and looked around. He was in a hole all right. Turtles aren't known to be the best climbers in the world, but Augie was tough, and he wasn't afraid. As far as he was concerned, this was just another adventure. Augie shook the dirt from his feet and slowly started to climb out of the hole. While trying to climb out, Augie wondered what his friends were doing.

Chapter 3

Harvey was working his way around a pile of firewood when he heard a car coming closer and closer. He turned around and saw a shiny brown car roll up to a stop in the driveway in front of the house. As soon as the car doors opened, two children came running out laughing and singing happy songs.

This commotion startled Defer and Hotie. They ran to the gate which was still opened and saw and heard the same things that Harvey did. They watched as the children and the adults emptied the car of all their suitcases, shopping bags, balls, games and books, and carried them into the little gray house with the cozy red chimney.

After everyone had gone into the house, Defer and Hotie came back through the gate and closed it behind them. Harvey jumped on Hotie's hoof and they all retraced their steps back to the hill near the house. When they reached the top of the hill, they looked around and waited for Augie to join them.

As they waited, they watched the little house come alive with activity. The children had put bathing suits on and were running towards the pool yelling, "the last one in the pool is a monkey's uncle!" The grownups finished unpacking the car and went into the backyard with the children.

Defer, Hotie, and Harvey waited and waited for Augie to make his way out of the backyard through one of the spaces in the bottom of the fence. They had no idea their turtle friend was in a hole trying to climb out!

Defer and Hotie started pacing back and forth as they waited. The longer they waited, the faster they paced. Faster and faster they went, until Defer turned around so quickly that he walked smack into Hotie and their heads came together with a clunk.

There was still no sign of Augie. While they waited, Augie's cousin Tyler came strolling by, slowly as turtles do, whistling a happy tune. (Tyler was always whistling. He whistled when he played, he whistled when he walked, and he whistled when he was sleeping. The only times he didn't whistle was when was eating.)

"What's up Hotie?" Tyler asked, as he nodded hello to Defer and Harvey. "We're all waiting for your cousin to come and join us," Hotie explained. "We were exploring a little while ago in the backyard of the little gray house over the hill, when the people who live there came home. We left quickly and seem to have left Augie behind. To tell you the truth, we're getting worried."

Tyler knew how slowly turtles do things and also knew his cousin better than most of his friends. Tyler and Augie grew up together in the same part of the forest. As Tyler whistled, he remembered some of the happy times he spent with Augie growing up and he recalled Augie's mother always telling him to hurry up. But Augie always used to say, "Don't worry mom, I'll get to it, it will just take me a little more time."

While all the friends were grouped together, Augie heard Tyler whistling. Augie knew that his friends were close by and he was not worried a bit. Augie whistled back to Tyler. (The two turtles had been whistling to each other since they were baby turtles.) Augie was still trying to climb out of that hole. He might be slow, but he wasn't a quitter. Each time he took a few steps up, he slid back down to the bottom of the hole.

Once they'd heard Augie's whistle, Tyler assured everyone that his cousin was okay.

The little group of friends began walking back to their homes. Defer and Hotie bumped into each other as they walked, and giggled each time. Tyler strolled along whistling a happy tune. Harvey had a bouncy ride in Tyler's hat, and found himself laughing as he rolled back and forth.

After a while, Augie got tired and hungry. Luckily, he remembered the honey and flowers under his shell and decided it was time for dinner. Augie cleared away some pebbles and began to prepare his dinner. He took a leaf and used it as a plate for his flowers and found an acorn shell and used it as a bowl for his honey. Augie was in pretty good spirits considering he was alone and it was starting to get dark, but he had faith that everything would turn out for the best. It always did. No matter how bad things looked, no matter how dark and dreary the evenings got, there was always tomorrow, and a new sunny day ahead filled with exciting adventures. Augie finished his dinner and put the leftover honey and flowers back under his shell.

As the darkness rolled in, the activity at the pool was beginning to quiet down. The children jumped in the pool for their last swim of the day.

Augie started to yawn. He decided to continue his climb in the morning when he hoped he would have an opportunity to meet and play with the children. With those pleasant thoughts, Augie pulled his back legs into his shell first, then his front legs, then his tail, and finally, after looking around and giving a small sigh, he pulled his head in. After only a moment, Augie was fast asleep, safe and snug in his own shell.

Augie had spent a quiet, peaceful night in his temporary home. As the sun began to rise, with the sweet smell of morning came music from the chirping of birds and the fluttering of butterflies. It was still too early for any activity from the people in the house... except for one.

Chapter 4

A little blonde boy named Josh was quietly listening to the sounds of nature from his bed. Josh liked to spend his early morning walking through the trees, talking to the birds and watching for the movement of all of the animals of the forest. On this very special morning, Josh lazily crawled out of bed, slid his feet into furry slippers which were too big for his feet, pulled his blue hooded sweatshirt off a hook next to his bed and tied it around his shoulders. Then, very quietly, he walked downstairs through the kitchen and into the backyard. He stopped by the holes he dug the previous week and considered planting one of his new bushes when he noticed something peculiar. There, sitting at the bottom of the hole, was a turtle shell in a pretty pattern of brown and green squares.

Josh wondered how the shell had gotten into the hole. As he looked closer, he noticed some movement. First a turtle's head peeked out of the shell, then one leg, then another and another and another, and finally a tail popped into view. Josh was so excited he could feel his heart pumping with joy. A new friend he thought. He could hardly contain his excitement, but he patiently waited for the turtle to wake up before he made any noise so as not to frighten him.

As Augie awoke slowly—breathing in the fresh air of the morning and shaking the sleep from his eyes— he sensed someone was watching him. He looked up and saw a little boy dressed in bright red and white striped pajamas, a blue sweatshirt and a wide, beaming smile. "Well, good morning," Josh said to Augie. "And good morning to you," Augie said introducing himself. "My name is Augie."

Josh was so very pleasantly surprised that he could understand turtle talk, that he could hardly get his words out. "G G Good morning, Augie," said the little boy, "my name is Josh". "Pleased to meet you," Augie replied. "Do you want to be in this hole?" Josh asked. "Would you like me to help you get out?"

"I sure would appreciate some assistance," Augie said with a sigh of relief. Very carefully, Josh picked Augie up by his shell and placed him gently on some leaves next to a tree nearby. Augie was very pleased with having the opportunity to walk about as he wished, instead of being stuck in the hole.

The two of them sat quietly for a moment looking at each other and smiling. Each realized they had made a new friend. They could just feel it. Augie told Josh how he ended up in the hole, about all his friends, and his whistling cousin, Tyler. Josh told Augie all about his family and friends, and how much he liked to whistle too, especially to the birds, and to have the birds whistle back to him.

What a great way to start the day! As the two new friends learned more and more about each other, they began to realize how much they liked each other. It was as if they had been pals for a long time. Josh and Augie had been talking for a while, sharing their stories as the morning sun grew bright, when they both heard noises coming from the house. The family was starting its day. Josh's sister, Rachael, was putting dishes on the table while Josh's mother was preparing breakfast.

"I've got a great idea," Josh said. "Why don't you come inside and have breakfast with me? I can introduce you to everyone, and after breakfast we can play. Are you hungry?" Augie thought for a moment. I am hungry, he said to himself. Josh is my friend, and I would like to meet his family and friends. "Sure," said Augie, "let's go."

Off they went, both smiling big wide smiles. Josh's mom was standing in the kitchen by the back door of the house and Josh's dad was walking down the stairs into the kitchen as they approached. "Guess what?" Josh asked as he walked in the door. "Have I got a surprise for you!" Josh turned around and pointed to the turtle making his way across the kitchen floor. "Meet my new friend Augie," he said with a very proud and pleased look on his face.

Josh's sister, and her mom and dad were always hearing guess what? from Josh. This time they felt there was something special like the time Josh came home with his sister's doll carriage filled with kittens. Or the time he came home with a shoe box full of baby chicks. They knew that this morning's guess what? was one of those "guess whats?" They all followed Josh's gaze to the floor and to their joyful surprise, they saw Augie, slowly walking into the house looking up at his new friend Josh. "Well, well," said Josh's mom. "Hot stuff," said Josh's dad. "Incredible," said Rachael.

"Breakfast is ready," Josh's mom announced. "Everyone, sit at the table, please." "You, too, Augie" Josh said. "You're the guest of honor!" Augie looked at all the food on the table. It was covered with cinnamon toast, rolls, scrambled eggs, milk, butter, jelly, honey, and cheese beautifully laid out on the table. They very politely, and with proper table manners, chose what they wanted and proceeded to eat a very hearty breakfast.

Everyone at the table thanked Josh's mom for a wonderful breakfast and asked how they could help in cleaning up. Josh carried the dirty dishes into the kitchen, Rachael washed the pans, Josh's dad washed the dishes and silverware, and Augie was given the job of drying the dishes. Josh's mom gave Augie a brand new dish towel that had a big, bright red rose on it. When Augie saw the flower, his eyes lit up. This was surely the biggest rose he had ever seen!

As the day wore on, Josh and Augie became even better friends. They did everything together. Josh and Augie returned to where they first met and planted a rose bush in the hole. Augie helped by covering the bush's roots with soil. Josh watered the flowers, bushes and trees in the garden while Augie stood behind Josh's legs so he wouldn't get all wet.

After everyone had finished their chores, it was time for a well deserved swim. Swimming was Augie's favorite activity, especially on such a bright, hot, sunny day. Josh and Rachael changed into their bathing suits and ran out to the pool. They took turns jumping off the diving board and trying to make the biggest splash possible. Augie crawled over to the steps of the pool and pushed himself into the water. He sighed a sigh of contentment as he soaked in the cool, refreshing water. Then Josh helped Augie onto one of the inflatable rafts and together they floated lazily on the water in the warm sunshine, totally enjoying the day and one another's company.

After a few moments, Josh broke the silence and said, "Augie, I've got a great idea. Why don't you come home to the city with us? You can live in my room with me, we can go to school together and you can meet my friends and teachers." Augie thought for a moment. Wow, would that be great! He thought about his friends and the forest and how much he would miss them. He thought about how much fun he was having. He knew he wouldn't leave without telling his friends where he was going. Augie finally said, "Josh, I'm going to take a walk in the woods and think about your friendly offer and we will talk when I come back."

Chapter 5

Josh picked Augie up and carried him to the edge of the pool where he gently placed him on the soft grass. Augie walked past the rows of beautiful flowers, past the tall trees and into the woods. As he made his way, he thought, and as he thought, he whistled. He thought about the times he and Tyler walked through the woods and whistled happy tunes. As they walked one rainy day, they whistled in the rain, and as they whistled, they danced. When they had finished their song and dance, they heard an audience of forest animals cheering and clapping for them from the trees.

Augie walked a bit more and decided to talk to his friends about Josh's invitation to go home to the city with him. When Augie returned home, all of his friends were waiting for him. They were smiling and so happy that he was finally home. Augie told them about Josh and his family and Josh's invitation. Tyler asked: "Why don't you visit for a little while and decide then? You don't have to make up your mind about living with Josh and his family now, do you?"

A sweet grin came across Augie's face. He stood straight up, kicked his feet together and said, "Wow, that's a great idea! That's what I can do!" He was so relieved. And to think that only a few moments before he was so troubled. "Everything turns out for the best," he said out loud. "Thanks for that great idea, Tyler." Augie felt fantastic. He strolled back to the pool whistling a very happy, perky tune. Josh heard him approach and waited for Augie to say something.

"Hi Josh," said Augie as he slowly slipped into the cool, clear, blue water of the pool. Augie asked Josh if he could go home with him for a visit first. Josh almost jumped out of the water in excitement. "Yippee!" he shouted. They both laughed and dove under water at the same time. They swam to the bottom of the pool, and jumped to the surface together. "What's all the excitement? " asked Rachael, as she turned lazily onto her back while sunning herself. "Guest what?" asked Josh. "What now?" Rachael answered. "Augie has accepted my invitation!" Josh said happily. "He's going to visit with us for a while."

The rest of the day was spent having fun and more fun. Augie and Josh swam together, had races in the pool and laughed together. Augie lost all of the races, but he beat Josh at floating. When Augie floated he just rolled onto his back. Josh thought his friend looked so funny with his four legs swinging in all directions that he laughed every time he looked at Augie, then Augie would laugh, too. The two new friends enjoyed each other's company and felt so good together, that their time together seemed to fly right by. When evening came Josh and Rachael left the pool and took showers before dinner. While they were bathing, Augie took a last swim by himself. How sweet the night air smelled to him, and how he looked forward to his upcoming adventure.

After a delightful dinner prepared by Rachael and her mom, everyone helped clean up. Most of the evening was taken up with quiet, restful activities. Josh's mom and Rachael read books, while Josh and Augie spent some quiet time looking at Josh's baseball card collection. After a while, Josh and Rachael stopped what they were doing because it was time for bed.

Rachael took her turn in the bathroom first. She washed her face. She washed her hands. She brushed her teeth. "All yours" she said to Josh when she was done.

Augie followed Josh into the bathroom and Josh sat him on the sink. Augie watched Josh brush his teeth. This was new to Augie but it seemed like a good idea. Maybe I should have a toothbrush, too? But what would I brush? he thought. Turtles don't have any teeth!

Josh's dad came home just in time to tuck Josh and Rachael into bed, kiss them goodnight and turn off the lights. Augie slept on a pillow next to Josh in bed. He knew the next day would be an exciting one. He fell asleep thinking about traveling to Josh's house, meeting new friends, and seeing new places. A little later on, Josh's dad went into Josh and Rachael's rooms as he did every night, to see if they were under the covers and to make sure everything was all right. As he turned around to leave Josh's room, he could see the smiles on both Josh and Augie's faces.

Morning arrived with sunlight streaming through the windows and skylights. The flowers and leaves had their faces turned toward the sun, each wearing a proud smile. Josh woke up first and watched as Augie stretched and yawned and rubbed the sleep from his eyes. Again, Augie awoke to find a smiling blonde boy next to him. "Good morning, Augie," Josh whispered. "Good morning, Josh," Augie replied.

The two pals rolled around in bed for a little while and giggled as they tickled each other. Rachael heard the laughter and came to see what was going on. Everyone was in a giggly mood. When she saw what was going on, she laughed too. All the laughter soon caught the attention of Josh's mom and dad. They, too, came in to see what was going on, and started laughing right along with everyone else.

"All right kids," said Josh's dad, "these are our plans for the morning: A quick, brisk swim followed by a light breakfast. You guys will help Mommy with cleaning up the house and I will water the garden and fill the bird feeder with bird seed. Then, it's into the car for a ride home to the city."

That is exactly what happened. Everyone put on a bathing suit— except Augie. As Augie was walking over to the pool, he wondered why people needed bathing suits. Augie thought that he was so very lucky that he had all the clothes he ever needed, right on his back. Josh, Rachael and Augie swam in the crisp morning sunshine, ate breakfast outside near the pool, and did their chores. After breakfast, Josh's dad helped clear the dishes from the table. Josh and Rachael helped wash the dishes and there was Augie, holding the dish towel with the big red rose just waiting to dry the wet, clean dishes.

Chapter 6

By 11:00 a.m., the house was locked up, the gate was closed, and the car was packed and ready to go. Josh's mom and dad were waiting by the car as Josh and Rachael came charging toward them. (It was tough to tell if Augie was charging or not. He might have thought he was, but it was hard to tell. We know how slowly turtles move, don't we?) Josh made room for Augie next to him in the back seat of the Betser. The trip home went by smoothly and quietly. Soft music played on the radio as everyone sat back, relaxed and enjoyed the passing scenery.

All of Augie's friends and cousin Tyler were very excited about Augie's trip to visit with Josh. They were all happy to hear that Augie made such nice, new friends.

Josh and his family lived in a big red brick apartment building that had a lot of apartments with a different family living in each one. Josh gave Augie plenty of time to get acquainted with the apartment in the city when they got home. Augie wandered around leisurely exploring every room. In Josh's room he found a fish tank with beautifully colored tropical fish. He knew that he would be spending a lot of time watching the fish swim around.

Since the next day was a school day, after dinner, Rachael and Josh sat down to do their homework. Augie felt left out because he wanted to do some homework, too. Josh saw that Augie wanted to do some work so he gave him a coloring book and some crayons. "Why don't you color a picture of a smiling clown with a big flower on his pointy hat?" Josh suggested. That seemed to satisfy Augie while Josh and Rachael finished their homework.

Josh thought about the best way to introduce Augie to his teacher and his friends. I'll just put Augie on Miss Rosalind's desk and really surprise everyone! he thought. After a few more wild ideas, he decided to introduce Augie properly. He would get into class early, greet his teacher with a friendly good morning, and tell her about his new pal. That seemed to be the best approach, and when he told his parents what he intended to do, they were very proud of him. They thought it was the most gentlemanly thing to do.

It was finally time for Josh, Rachael and Augie to go to sleep. Josh's mom and dad came in to check on everyone and Josh's mom gave everyone a kiss goodnight—even Augie. Augie was so surprised and happy with the kiss that he blushed. (Did you ever see a turtle blush?) Augie's face turned pink and he grinned a little turtle grin as he fell asleep next to Josh.

29

The big day arrived. Augie and Josh were awakened by a buzzing sound. Augie was so startled by the loud noise, that he pulled his head, tail and all four of his legs into his shell in the blink of an eye. He couldn't figure out what the noise was until Josh explained to him what an alarm clock was and how it was used. Augie never needed anything like that to wake him up in the morning—the chirping of the birds always woke him.

Augie watched as Josh washed his hands and face, brushed his teeth and got dressed for school. When he was done, the two friends went into the kitchen for breakfast. Josh shared his cereal, milk, and honey—drizzled toast with his pal. As each moment went by, Augie's excitement grew and grew. Josh gathered his school books and put Augie on his shoulder. "Hold on," Josh said to Augie, "we're on our way."

Chapter 7

The walk to school was nice and quiet. On the way, they met a sweet, smiling, blue eyed classmate of Josh's. She was walking to school, skipping with every step. "Hi, Josh," she squeaked in a happy voice. "Hi, Reeva," Josh replied. "I'd like to introduce my friend Augie to you." Reeva hadn't noticed Augie sitting on Josh's shoulder. When she saw him, she jumped backwards and laughed out loud. "Wow, he's beautiful. I'm pleased to meet you," she said, looking directly into his eyes with her nose almost touching Augie's nose.

Reeva, Josh and Augie continued walking together the rest of the way to school, up the stairs and into their classroom. Their teacher, Ms. Rosalind, was preparing some arithmetic problems on the blackboard as Josh and Reeva walked in. "Good morning, Ms. Rosalind," they sang together. As Ms. Rosalind turned toward Josh and Reeva, she said, "and good mor......" and suddenly stopped, and stared at Augie. Augie looked back at her and sort of smiled at Ms. Rosalind. After a few seconds and still very surprised, Ms. Rosalind said, "Yes, and good morning to you, too. What a lovely surprise. Who is your friend?" Before Josh could say anything, Reeva blurted, "This is Augie. Josh met him a few days ago in the country and. . . . ." "Slow down, slow down," Ms. Rosalind whispered. "Josh, why don't you tell me about your four legged friend." "Well," Josh said, "his name is Augie and he really is my pal. We do everything together. I found him in a hole in the backyard of my country house this past weekend, and he came to visit with me this week."

"Why, that's wonderful," said Ms. Rosalind. "You can introduce your new friend to the class. Why don't you put Augie near the window until everyone else gets here?" From the window Augie could see the schoolyard filled with Josh's classmates who were all running around and playing games.

Ms. Rosalind went to the back of the classroom and pulled on a rope that was attached to a bell. As she pulled the rope, the bell began to clang. That was the signal for the children to stop playing and come into the classroom. When the entire class was seated, Miss Rosalind said, "Class, Josh has a surprise for you this morning. He has a special friend he would like you to meet." At that moment, Josh walked over to the window and moved some books. Right behind them stood Augie, his head up high and his shell glistening in the morning sun as it streamed through the window. "Here he is, class; my new friend, Augie", said Josh triumphantly.

As if rehearsed, the entire class OOHED and AAHED. All of the children crowded around the window to get a closer look. The next few minutes were spent with Josh's classmates asking Josh questions and playing with Augie. That's when Augie noticed something very strange, something he had never seen before. One of the boys was chewing something, and all of a sudden, a big pink bubble came out of his mouth. The bubble kept getting bigger and bigger until it exploded. Augie was so startled he rolled over onto his shell and he couldn't get up. Josh gave Augie a little nudge to help him roll over and get back on all four legs.

"What was that pink stuff?" Augie asked. How do you blow bubbles with it? Augie wondered. "It's called bubble gum" Josh told him. Josh thought for a few seconds and gave Augie a piece of bubble gum. "You chew until it's soft, then you kind of poke a dent in it with your tongue and just blow" Josh explained." What a funny sight—a little brown turtle chewing bubble gum and blowing bubbles. There was one problem with all this—Augie didn't know how to stop. The bubble got bigger and bigger and bigger until it popped. There was pink bubble gum all over Augie's face and shell. He was so surprised when it popped that he pulled in his head and all four legs in a flash. The entire class laughed and laughed. Slowly, Augie poked his head out and then his legs. It took Josh and Reeva ten minutes to get the gum off Augie's face and shell.

Now it was time for learning. Ms. Rosalind asked the students in the class to sit in their seats and asked Augie if he would like to sit on her desk while she taught the day's lesson. Augie realized this was a special honor and accepted her invitation proudly. That morning, Augie learned how to add numbers together that added up to seven—even if he didn't exactly know what a seven was. After the lesson, it was time for lunch. At this time, the entire class went to the lunchroom to eat. First, they sang some songs and then ate lunch. The folks who were in charge of the lunchroom prepared a special meal for Augie. While all of Josh's classmates ate tuna fish sandwiches, fruit and milk, Augie feasted on fresh lettuce and crunchy crackers. After lunch, the children sang more songs and then returned to class.

That afternoon, Ms. Rosalind taught a lesson on nature, in Augie's honor. He was pleasantly surprised to find he knew a lot about the lesson. He even knew enough to answer one of the questions that Ms. Rosalind asked the class. When school was over for the day, each one of Josh's classmates came over to play with Augie. And that's the way it went for the whole school week. Augie met all of Josh's friends, learned a lot about many things, and was treated as a friend by everyone he met.

Chapter 8

In the late afternoon and evenings, Josh and Augie spent all of their time together—sometimes with Rachael and Josh's mom and dad and sometimes with Reeva—but always together. After a few days, all of Josh's friends had heard about Josh and his new friend. In the mornings on the way to school, the shopkeepers would wait for Josh and Augie to pass by to say hello. Near school, there was a new building being built. When the two friends passed by, the construction workers would always say hi, and Eddie, the crane operator would toot his horn and say good morning. What wonderful feelings Augie had about his new friends. They were so nice to him. They always had something cheery to say, and always smiled.

After school, Josh and Augie met the mommies and daddies who came to pick up their children. Some of the parents had babies with them. Augie loved to see the babies and play with them. They gurgled and smiled at him while he whistled and smiled back at them. That made them gurgle and smile even more. The babies loved it when Augie pulled his head inside his shell. When he pulled his head in, there was a silent look of surprise on the baby's face, and when he popped his head back out, the babies would screech with excitement and laughter.

Augie's visit in the city with Josh was coming to a close. The school week was over and the next day, Augie, Josh, Rachael and Josh's mom and dad would be going back to their country house for the weekend. That night, Augie spent some quiet time by himself watching the colorful fish swim around in Josh's fish tank. Even though he'd spent such a fantastic, wonderful, fun filled, happy few days with Josh and his family and friends, Augie knew, deep down inside, he was a forest turtle. He missed his friends, his cousin Tyler and the forest. Augie knew how very lucky he was to have had the chance to meet new friends, to learn lessons in school, and see so many new things. It was as if he was specially chosen from all the forest animals to have these experiences, but he felt it was time to join his forest friends again. At the same time, though, Augie knew he would miss Josh and his family and friends very much— especially Josh.

What to do? he asked himself. All of a sudden, an idea came to him! Augie realized he didn't have to choose after all! Josh and his family come to the country often enough, he said to himself. I can go home to the forest and Tyler and my friends, and Josh can visit me. "What a terrific idea!" he exclaimed. At that point, one of the goldfish in the fish tank looked at Augie with a very puzzled look. It was as if the fish was asking: Who is this turtle talking to?

Augie walked over to Josh as he was adding up more numbers, making more sevens. He still didn't know what a seven was, but that was okay. The two friends spoke for a while. Augie told Josh how much he missed Tyler and his animal friends. He also told Josh how good he felt when he was with him. Josh tried to put himself in Augie's place and understand how his pal felt. Then and there they agreed to always be friends and visit each other whenever possible.

Night had fallen during their conversation, and it was time to go to sleep. Josh jumped into bed while Augie crawled over to his special place nearby. A pleasant, peaceful sleep came to these two close friends. They dreamt of their friendship and their happy times together. Even in their dreams, they had each other.

The next morning everyone in Josh's house rose early. The family packed the car, and soon, they were on their way to the country house. They were greeted by sunshine and pretty blue butterflies when they arrived. Some of the butterflies fluttered around Josh and tickled his ears, but most fluttered around Augie. It was their way of welcoming him back to the forest. The butterflies had missed Augie very much while he was visiting the city. The sweet country air filled Augie's senses with joy. Augie couldn't wait to see Tyler and his friends and tell them about his wonderful adventures. Before he knew it, Augie heard a familiar whistle coming from the forest. He knew it was Tyler's whistle, but he wondered how Tyler knew he was returning just then.

Augie thanked Josh and his family for a terrific visit and promised to see them again soon. Josh stayed by Augie's side as he walked toward the trees. As they entered the forest, they were met by Tyler, Hotie, Defer, and Harvey all dressed in party hats made from folded lily pads. His friends and cousin had gotten together to welcome Augie home with a party.

Augie told them about the great times he had on his visit with Josh and his family. They invited Josh to come along to the party. At the end of the party, Josh gave Augie a big hug and said goodbye to everyone and returned to his country house. As Josh walked, he whistled and on his face was the biggest smile he ever had, thinking about the great times he had with his new friend, Augie the turtle.

About the Author

My career started out as a Math teacher working with Junior High school students in Brooklyn, New York. For many years I have tutored children of all ages from Kindergarten through high school that needed support in Math.

I have always had a special place in my heart for children of all ages but especially younger children. Fortunate to marry young and to have had children at an early age, our children enjoyed skiing during the winter months in the Pocono mountains. My wife and I watched from inside the ski lodge. It was there my first thoughts began to write a children's story book and that is how Augie was born.

The idea was to get children excited about listening to and learning to read books. Our own children went to bed each evening after listening to a book read to them until they were old enough to read to themselves. To this day, we all still end our days reading a bit. We consider books to be like good friends!

Having worked my way through corporate America as an IT manager, I put aside my first book for about 25 years always thinking about the time when I would be able to sit down and finish my first Augie's Adventure in the City book.

My own children are grown and my wife and I now find the time to "stop and smell the roses."

Augie's Adventures in the City is the first book in a series I hope to continue where children will feel joy, learn consideration, feel empathy, and generally come to learn to love reading for what it is-- an adventure, always an adventure of some kind.

Made in the USA
Las Vegas, NV
10 May 2021

22801334R00031